FoolsCap in association with Soho

SPINE
BY CLARA BRENNAN

Cast

Amy: **Rosie Wyatt**

Creative Team

Director: **Bethany Pitts**

Producer: **Francesca Moody**

Designer: **Alison Neighbour**

Lighting Designer: **Fridthjofur Thorsteinsson**

Sound and Music: **Jon McLeod**

Stage Manager: **Anna Hunscott**

Assistant Lighting Designer: **Carrie Lonsdale**

PR: **Chloe Nelkin Consulting**

Spine premiered in Underbelly on 31 July 2014 as part of the
Edinburgh Frin⟨...⟩ ⟨...⟩ated as part of
Theatre Uncut i⟨...⟩

CAST AND CREATIVE TEAM

Clara Brennan (Writer)
Clara won the Channel 4 Playwright award for her forthcoming play *The Vendor* and is resident at the Soho Theatre for 2014. She received the Off West End Adopt a Playwright Award in 2012. Previous work includes *Bud Take the Wheel, I Feel a Song Coming On* (Underbelly); Theatre Uncut plays *Hi Vis* (Southwark Playhouse, Teatre Lliure), *Spine* (Young Vic) and *The Wing* (Young Vic); *Monogram* (Cockpit Theatre); *Rain* as part of *Lough/Rain* (Underbelly/York Theatre Royal); *Portmanteau* (Bike Shed Theatre); and *Births, Marriages and Deaths* (High-Hearted Theatre). She has film and television series in development. A reading of her new play *Boa* starring Dame Harriet Walter premiered at the HighTide Festival 2014.

Rosie Wyatt (Amy)
Rosie trained at Royal Welsh College of Music and Drama. Theatre includes: *Worst Wedding Ever* (Salisbury Playhouse); *Blink* (Traverse, Edinburgh/Soho Theatre/Jagriti Theatre, India – for nabokov); *Virgin* (Watford Palace); *One Man, Two Guvnors* (National and International Tour for the National Theatre); *Mogadishu* (UK tour and Lyric Hammersmith); *Bunny* (Fringe First Winner. Underbelly, Edinburgh/UK tour/Soho Theatre/59E59, New York – for nabokov); *Love Love Love* (UK tour for Paines Plough and Plymouth Drum). Television includes: *New Tricks* and *Doctors*. Radio includes: *Pride and Prejudice*.

Bethany Pitts (Director)
Bethany Pitts is a theatre director specialising in new work, both scripted and devised, and has trained in directing with Katie Mitchell, Di Trevis, Lyndsey Turner, Told By An Idiot and through the Young Vic Director's Network. She was Assistant Director at Theatre Royal Plymouth from 2012–2013, working under Artistic Director Simon Stokes, and prior to that worked as Resident Assistant Director at Theatre503. She co-runs the MolinoGroup for whom directing includes *DESERT* (National Tour/Latitude Festival) and *The Roland Piece* (Bike Shed Theatre

/Rosemary Branch). Freelance directing credits include *Acres* (New Diorama); *The Caravan* (ParkTheatre); *The Neighbour* (Arcola) and assisting includes *Theatre Uncut* at the Young Vic, *Dark Vanilla Jungle* by Philip Ridley (Soho/Pleasance – Fringe First winner 2013); *Forever House* by Glenn Waldron; and *The Astronaut's Chair* by Rona Munro (Drum Plymouth). She directed the short version of *Spine* for Theatre Uncut Plymouth in 2012.

Francesca Moody (Producer)
Francesca is currently the Assistant Producer at Paines Plough. She is also the Producer for DryWrite and an associate at Undeb Theatre, SEArED Productions and Look Left Look right. In 2013 two of her productions at the Edinburgh Festival were awarded Fringe Firsts. Her freelance credits include *Home* (SEArED/Arcola); *Fleabag* (DryWrite/Soho Theatre/Underbelly); *Gardening: For the Unfulfilled and Alienated* (Undeb/Pleasance); *Where The White Stops* (Antler/Underbelly); *Jekyll & Hyde* (Flipping the Bird/Assembly/Southwark Playhouse); *Mydidae* (DryWrite/Soho Theatre/Trafalgar Studios); *JOE/BOY* (We Were here/The Last Refuge); *Chamber of Curiosities*, *Not Another Musical*, *The Welsh Atlantis* (Latitude Festival); *You Once Said Yes* (Look Left Look Right/The Roundhouse/LIFT Festival/Lowry), *NOLA* (Underbelly/Escalator East to Edinburgh); and *Brimstone and Treacle* (Arcola Theatre).

Alison Neighbour (Designer)
Alison trained as a designer at RADA. She designs for theatre and events in site specific and traditional settings, and occasionally for film and TV. Theatre includes: *I Told You This Would Happen* (ARC, Stockton & touring); *Wedding* (Shoreditch Town Hall); *Square Bubble* (National Theatre Watch This Space); *The Eyes Have It* (Imagine Watford); Spectra (mac, Birmingham); *Romeo & Juliet Unzipped* (Salisbury Playhouse & Bath Egg); *Followers* (Southwark Playhouse); *Used Blood Junkyard* (Arcola); *A Conversation* (tour); *Late in the Day* (Hen & Chickens); *Show in a Shop Window* (Daggett Gallery); *That's The Way To Do It* (tour); *Le Peau de Chagrin* (Holland Park); *Harmless Creatures* (Hull Truck/Greyscale); *Oh, To Be In England* (Finborough);

Childsplay (tour); *The Fall of the House of Usher* (Dalston Boys Club); *Gloucestershire* (Arcola), *Never Any Fruit* (Pleasance Islington); *Love Horse* (White Bear). Events & Spaces: The Literary Ball (L'Institut Francais); Swingtime Casino (The Roost, Gingerline); Puppeteer Workshop (Canvas & Cream, Gingerline); Victorian Christmas (Brunel Museum, Gingerline); Tate Britain Watercolours Film & Music Event (Latitude Festival); Theatre Brothel (Northern Stage, Hull Truck, Almeida, Greyscale); The Shunt Yard (Shunt Collective). Alison is also co-artistic director of Bread & Goose, for whom she has designed: *The Incurable Imagination of Anthony Jones* (Wales Millennium Centre & Camden People's Theatre); *Stations By Heart* (St Pancras station); *Mission: A Stranger's Promise* (Camden People's Theatre); *Mission: It Has Begun* (Scarborough town centre); *Fox in the Snow* (Brixton market). Alison's scenographic work for *The Incurable Imagination of Anthony Jones* was shown at the 2013 World Stage Design Festival.

Fridthjofur Thorsteinsson *(Lighting Designer)*
Fridthjofur – better known as Fiffi – studied lighting design at The Central School of Speech and Drama (BA Hons '09) and scenography at Central St. Martin's College of Art and Design (MA'13). He has worked in theatre, opera, ballet, dance, musicals, fashion and events in the UK, Iceland and in Europe – including Ireland, Sweden, Germany, Estonia and more. Past lighting designs include *Julius Caesar*, *The Impostor* and *The Good Soul of Szechwan* for Drama Centre London; *Heaven* in Berlin for Hobo Theatre; *Blackout* for Theatre Mogul (IS); *Carmen* for Impact Opera company; a *Bacchae* for Yard Theatre; *Just Here* for S.Ingadottir (dance); *Fresh Meat* for S.Ingadottir & S.Nielsdottir (dance); *Trudleikur*, *Godir Halsar* and *Hetja* for Frystiklefinn (IS); *The Screams of Kitty Genovese* for Single Malt Productions and more. Fiffi also works as a theatre consultant for Theatre Projects Consultants in London. For further information and photographs, please visit http://fif.fi

Jon McLeod (Sound and Music)
Sound and music credits include *A Conversation*, *Party Skills for the End of The World* (Nigel Barrett and Louise Mari); *66 Minutes in Damascus* (LIFT Festvial); *In the Neuron Forest*, *Terminus Treats*, *The Eyes Have It* (Bread & Goose); *In This Place* (Pentabus Theatre); *The Invisible Show* (RedShift Theatre); *In the Neuron Forest*, *Terminus Treats*, *The Eyes Have It* (Bread & Goose); *Square Bubble*, *The Match* (Marianne Badrichani); *Nightmare Dreamer*, *Flying Roast Goose* (Blue Elephant); *The Fanny Hill Project* (Theatre State); *Borderline Vultures* (The Lowry); *Headspace*, *Waiting Game*, *Nana's Jumble* (Kazzum), *To Close Your Eyes Is To Travel* (The Yard); *XY, Cut Off, I Still Get Excited When I See a Ladybird* (Theatre503). As associate sound designer; *Damned By Despair* (National Theatre). Jon's play *Organs of Little Apparent Importance* was produced for HighTide Festival Theatre.

Anna Hunscott (Stage Manager)
Anna is really looking forward to returning to the Edinburgh Fringe Festival which she has been attending for over 10 years. Since graduation from the London Academy of Music and Dramatic Arts she has worked with Paines Plough on *Wasted* and *Hopelessly Devoted* by Kate Tempest and in venues such as the Birmingham Rep, Roundhouse, Sherman Theatre and The Tricycle.

FoolsCap

Foolscap was set up in 2014 by Francesca Moody, Bethany Pitts and Clara Brennan to craft politically conscious new work with storytelling at its heart. We are passionate about galvanising audiences, through a combination of grit, wit and great theatre.

FoolsCap would like to thank the following people and organisations without whom this production would not have been possible. Steve Marmion, Mark Godfrey, David Luff, Nina Steiger and all at Soho Theatre, Marina Dixon, Fiona McCurdy and all at Underbelly, Helen Murray, Giles Moody, Theatre Uncut, Theatre Royal Plymouth, Connie Pankhurst, Scenery Salvage, Lesoco and Moria Tighe, Carol Tambor, Simon Stokes, Hannah Price, Emma Callander and all at Theatre Uncut, David Greig, David Prescott, Christina Burnett, Clare Suart, Jessica Cooper, Kat Buckle, Camilla Young and all at Curtis Brown, Annie Back, Frances McIvor, Anna Morris, Beth Vyse, Holli Dempsey, Luke Barnes, George Spender and all at Oberon Books.

London's most vibrant venue for new theatre, comedy and cabaret.

Soho Theatre is a major creator of new theatre, comedy and cabaret. Across our three different spaces we curate the finest live performance we can discover, develop and nurture. Soho Theatre works with theatre makers and companies in a variety of ways, from full producing of new plays, to co-producing new work, working with associate artists and presenting the best new emerging theatre companies that we can find. We have numerous writers and theatre makers on attachment and under commission, six young writers and comedy groups and we read and see hundreds of shows a year – all in an effort to bring our audience work that amazes, moves and inspires.

'Soho Theatre was buzzing, and there were queues all over the building as audiences waited to go into one or other of the venue's spaces. [The audience] is so young, exuberant and clearly anticipating a good time.' *Guardian*

We attract over 170,000 audience members a year.

We produced, co-produced or staged over forty new plays in the last twelve months.

Our social enterprise business model means that we maximise value from Arts Council and philanthropic funding; we actually contribute more to government in tax and NI than we receive in public funding.

SOHOTHEATRE.COM

Keep up to date:
sohotheatre.com/mailing-list
facebook.com/sohotheatre
twitter.com/sohotheatre
youtube.com/sohotheatre

SPINE

Clara Brennan

SPINE

OBERON BOOKS
LONDON

WWW.OBERONBOOKS.COM

First published in 2014 by Oberon Books Ltd
521 Caledonian Road, London N7 9RH
Tel: +44 (0) 20 7607 3637 / Fax: +44 (0) 20 7607 3629
e-mail: info@oberonbooks.com
www.oberonbooks.com

A catalogue record for this book is available from the British
Library.

PB ISBN: 978-1-78319-166-6
E ISBN: 978-1-78319-665-4

Cover photograph by Helen Murray

Printed and bound by Marston Book Services, Didcot.

For my uncle, Andy Helliker.
To Sue and Joshua with all my love.

Dusk in the front room of a mews house in London. Silhouettes of mysterious household clutter behind AMY, a teenage girl.

She is alone in the house, but impersonates GLENDA, an elderly cockney woman. She does not have to be excellent at mimicry but does enjoy doing it.

Text in italics indicates when she speaks in the voice of GLENDA.

AMY: I rock up on her doorstep and she opens the door.

She's a shrunken little biddy with shocking died red hair. And she's standin' there in nothing but a negligee, a cream silk one. And round her ankles are baggy beige pop socks, not pulled up. She's lookin' up at me…but she doesn't seem to clock I got a massive fuckin' shiner and dried blood all down my top.

Instead of slammin' the door in my face she turns round to lead me into the house and I see there's this little smudge of shit on the back of her nightie, and I think, that's the saddest…that's like the most vulnerable thing I ever saw.

An' anyway she says, *'I can't show you the room meself 'cause I live downstairs and I've got a home help comes three times a week but she's gone for the day'*……and oh my god!

Looking round as she bangs on, the place is a shit hole, big and everything, massive old house, but it's – a mess, not like, of dirt, but of stuff, years full of stuff! Worthless fuckin' knickknacks, everywhere!

And she says, *'I can't get up them stairs, it's my knee you see.'* And she's saying all sorts of random shit like. She's the widow of a man called Louie, and she said he died upstairs, having a tug of his 'clickety click.' You <u>what?</u>

'Ooh I hadn't heard a peep out of him for a few hours, so I struggles up them stairs and I find him there, dead to the world! Caught 'im with 'is trousers down, well an' truly, I can tell you! Sat at 'is bureau desk with a lingerie catalogue opened up in front of 'im, trousers down round 'is ankles an' ever such a look o' surprise on 'is face!

I'll say that for 'im, my Louie was a real go-er! He was stiff as a board, stiff as anything!'

Oh my god, this is fuckin' sick. She's actual nuts.

'But don't be a-feared my gel, 'e's too embarrassed to be a ghost.'

She gives me this big cold Victorian key, and says first floor, second door on the right, that's the room. And I go up her stairs thinking what the fuck am I doing here? She's talked me into – I think I ain't taking

the room, I've been blown off course by this
gross old bird, what the fuck am I doin'?

But I'm climbin the stairs in-I?

I go into a back bedroom, and it's got two
doors coming off it. It's got this big what
you call a bureau desk in it –an' the top of
the desk has like, an eyelid, the roller bit is
rolled back, so the desktop's thick with dust.
An' there are fingerprints around a leather
rectangle, and a proper old ink well, like
fuckin' hell this is where the old bloke died!
Fuckin' 'ell if I stay ere any longer I'm gonna
be stuck in the Victorian times! And this –
now – is when I get cold. A chill just rises up
from my ankles, and I shudder. I shudder.

Look on another day I might have turned
the room over and rinsed the place but this
is some creepy-ass shit –

There's something's <u>there.</u>

I leg it back downstairs, start making my
excuses but she's got the damn kettle on
and keeps me there, draws me back to the
kitchen, says she's got *'things she wants to ask
me,'* she puts cloths down as stepping stones
on the tiles because she's just mopped it,
and she leans on the kitchen table in front of

me, makes me sit at it. And I do. 'Cause I'm
fuckin' knackered.

And slowly she puts her little leg up on
a stool and rolls up these tan pop socks,
and I remember thinking 'Ames mate, this
cannot get any weirder', 'cause it's like she
didn't know who I was suddenly? And
she's leaning down and slowly, ever-so-
slowly pulling up this tan pop-sock up her
shin, rollin' it up like she's a stripper and
she's pulling on her sexy time stockins! It's
properly a bit sexual or something! Like
maybe she was a right babe in her day you
know? I think she was; I think maybe she
was.

But – <u>rank!</u> She's got bandages covering the
oozing of her varicose veins just like my Nan
did! Except I'm here with an old bird I don't
know, in her underwear!

And this is when she turns and looks at my
black eye, like she only just seen it. And she
says: *'Don't tell me you walked into a door.'*

An' I dunno what it is, I just start talkin', just
to like, <u>not watch</u> her, I go an' start the whole
story of…

Well my ex-best mate Faye, yeah, texts me
about some guy she's just met, and he's

apparently sent her pictures of his knob.
And she says they're not even good pics,
you can just see a Sky Sports menu in the
background and his little willy lollin' about
in front of a flat screen? So she texts me
LOLROTFWMLITA, which is 'Laughing
Out Loud Rollin On The Floor With My
Legs In The Air'. You'd have to meet her but
she's got this way of deliverin' a punchline
with this really serious face on her, and it
kills me. Anyway, my nine year-old sister
enjoys pointin' out it's an ACRONYM.

Faye an' me. We're in what from the
outside, to the untrained eye what might
look like a girl gang. Until I meet this knob-
photographer she's on about: Swanny.

He drives after me that day and he's all
like 'Baby girl, how can I get to know you?'
And I'm like. I stop dead, right by his car,
and I go: 'Trust me, you don't wanna know
me.' An' he keeps drivin' round the blocks
til I get to my estate and I'm like, 'This is
stalking.' We end up going for a wine and
he's acting all machismo, talking about his
job at a garage and how's he a kick boxer
and that? Anyway, he says he can teach me
self-defence, and we start off sorta, well from
that day on me going to the club, watching
him in the ring, and then him for a laugh
gettin' the pads out and getting me to punch

at 'im? And I gotta say, it feels pretty good punchin' the shit outta them pads. I'm a southpaw, and yeah I'm weak as fuck at first, but I get well into it. And then soon we're like, watching *Enter the Dragon* – and he teaches me Wing Chun.

So it starts with Swanny as like, my mentor. Now Wing Chun's what like, Ip Man taught to Bruce Lee, and it's perfect for little people. 'Cause instead of swingin' a punch and leaning back to assess your next move, it's close range. Meanin' you just like, barrel into someone – you move forward. And you keep goin, punch punch punch punch punch into the person! It's all about having the courage to move into the fight rather than swing and come out? It takes GUTS. And importantly, while you're barreling in like Bruce, you gotta remember to punch THROUGH THE PERSON. And I get pretty good at it, gotta say. And for like, three months? We're just mates. Until this one day when I stay over.

But he's already started slaggin' the way I dress, sayin I'm too old now to be wearin' jeans and jumper, and I say yeah well I don't need to wear a bodycon dress to feel sexy, and he says yeah but there are ways of wearin' jeans and a jumper, and I near put five across his face then. But I take it, and I keep on takin' it, until finally I know it ain't healthy to be around him. I start feelin' a knot in my stomach all day and I know I'm not concentrating: he's got this hold over me.

I remember looking in his bathroom mirror thinking, this is it, Ames, you're about to lose your cherry.

Back in his room it's hot as, and I'm tired. I'm physically dog-tired, and it's all a hot blur really. He kisses me and he does this thing where he rolls his tongue into a little point, and it's darting in and out my mouth, poke poke poke. I feel a bit sick! If he can't kiss what the hell is this going to be like?

And the simple answer is: it's all about him, there's no interest from him in me, y'know, getting off! Like I'm just a hole. Man! The way he ties a little knot in the condom and swaggers to the bin, with this little serious face goin' like this, *(Frowns, mimes tying a knot.)* like that cum's so precious, like that shit is gold dust, like it's going to escape and race back up my fanny!

But this in't even the worse bit.

He wants a second go at it and uhhh! He's on top of me and he – well he's startin' to talk what I think he thinks is dirty talk, and then – he proper slaps me on the fanny!

He spanks my fanny! And as he does it he shouts: 'Ah <u>OWN</u> that pussy!' And for a second I am stunned. I. Am. Stunned.

Stunned like. I'm looking up at him like, 'What the shit in hell, WAS THAT?'

He might as well have shouted, 'Show me the money!' So I slap him back! First I slap his cock with the back of my hand – doosh! – out the way! Then I get up and slap his face OFF his face! A proper stinger! And I'm on the other side of the room pullin' my clothes on and I'm like, are you having a fucking laugh? You moron! And he's butt naked going: 'Babe, where you goin'?' and I turn to him and go:

'No one. And I mean no one but me. Owns MY VAGINA!' Yeah! Proper like whooot!

Then I am out the door!

I'm like, glad I got it out the way but seriously, I ain't doin' that again until I'm like, twenty-six at least. Seriously, number one rule should be if he kisses real good then he's got some sensitivity. Number two is, he should probly be keen to make sure you have some pleasure. So if you're all getting down to it and the bloke's got no interest in touching you, if he's not feedin' the pony, pack up and go home ladeez!

Next day I tell Faye and the girls at school, but they cuss me. They're like, 'That is dirty! What you doing going with a guy like him? He's ten years older than you, you should know better!'

So I'm tellin' the old biddy how, from that day? Faye just drops me as her best friend.

I'm fuckin' cast out! I'm treated like proper filth. When they ain't ignorin' me they call me 'slag' and 'ho' and proper disown me!

'They sent you to Coventry,' says the old bird. Er, well no, they dint, but all right.

I end up with Es in my A levels. I reckon about that time I start to be a bit of a handful at home. Me and my Stepdad Jase, we start properly bangin' heads.

I get this job at a hair salon. I got no idea what to do with my life. Sweeping up dead hair, supposedly apprenticed but they teach me fuck all.

I dint last long. Here's what happens. And I gotta frame it, so I go to the old dear – and this makes her laugh: Fing about periods is, no one thinks to tell you about the shits. I never got told! I get the shits real bad when I'm 'on'. So this day I'm out the back of the hair salon on the cazi, just willing my bowels to stop exploding, thinking who'd be a woman, eh?!

I was only in there for five minutes, but when I come out the shop is in a <u>major panic</u>, 'cause it turns out…I had the stopwatch with me in the loo.

And this posh woman's colours – t-bar highlights and an all over tint, have been left on too long. I mean like, long enough for the strands to break off. I can see – patches of her scalp. So, yeah. All the stylists are suddenly lookin at me about to tear strips off me.

An' here's the thing. I don't suffer fools. So I'm like, 'It was an accident!' But the customer wants to sue their arses – so in front of her, the dickheads fire me! And to put it mild – I fuckin flip the fuck out!

I lean over the receptionist and my arm's just sweepin like that – hwaaaanggg – rows and rows of hair product onto the floor! And then I get the big glass dish of individually wrapped peppermints that are for CLIENTS ONLY, and I dooooosh that dish onto the floor! And then I get my bag *(Snaps her fingers, scowl face.)* and walk out.

And I'm fuckin' wound up, walking through a sea of commuters, feeling a bit dizzy, my womb is throbbing, and I'm thinking how I'm still owed last week's forty quid, and what am I gonna do? I'm suddenly callin' Swanny. Moment of fuckin' weakness.

I skip this bit for the old girl yeah – but while I'm waitin' for him I go in to a makeup counter and I use the sleeve of my coat to like, hoover up a couple of kohl pencils and a lipliner?

So next, I say to her: Swanny takes me to the pub. And lo and behold the girls I went to school with are all there eye-ballin' me, watchin' me neckin' the shots he's buying me, 'cause I wanna get <u>blotto</u>, I wanna get <u>wrecked.</u>

I'm headin' to the loos at one point and Faye's goin' in too, and that's when it happens.

'You're a filthy slag,' says Faye. I eyeball her. 'That the best you can do?' But then she goes: 'Your family's a bunch of pikeys.' And all the other girls laugh at me.

I'm everyone's mate until they prove themselves not to be. Serious, I love people, straight up. But you cross me, and –

'cause, oh fuck me mate: this gets worse.

'cause obviously I know martial arts. And I just see red.

Remember Ames, while you're barreling in like Bruce, you gotta remember to punch THROUGH THE TARGET.

If there was a slow-mo of it you'd probly see I illustrated the principles of centre line and simultaneous attack and defence to a fuckin' T.

The other girls are tryin' to pull me off, and Swanny gets involved at the last minute but I'm already on the floor takin' a kickin' and Faye's fallen down next to me and a strip of her false eyelashes flutters down, and I catch it in my palm like a black butterfly – and I black out then, I reckon.

Now I ain't proud of it. I ain't. I want like, meaning to hurt her.

'Course you wont meanin' to hurt her, you was upset, she was your best friend!' Yeah. *'But, you knew she liked him. This Swanny.'*

(Beat. AMY opens her mouth to deny this, but closes it.)

Basically I lose my job, I get fired, on account of my uterus wall lining falling away. And then I get harassed by bully girls and deck my best mate since birth.

So I'm spillin' this little biddy my whole story – I mean, she ain't gonna give me the room now! But she starts talkin' about the house. So I stop an' listen –

'We been in this 'ouse for a hundred and thirty-eight years!'

And I'm like, er, you can't have been.

'My grandparents came here on their wedding day. The Mountjoy's on Fitzroy Avenue bought it for 'em. Millionaires, they were. She entered their house as a scullery maid and he as a server. Ended up as head parlour girl and he head butler. We been in this house for a hundred and thirty-eight years!'

She gets out this crockery and gives me a cup and saucer.

'You got family?'

Yeah I got people. But they're kickin' me out. 'cause of my behaviour.

Last night after this set-to with Faye and the
girls, Swanny drives me home.

I get home and my mum's waitin' up for me.

The first thing I see on the kitchen table
in front of her are these letters headed
WONGA and my heart sorta drops into my
stomach. What you borrowin' more money
for? On top o' that she's borrowed £100
quid at 55 per cent interest from a loan shark
for my sister's birthday. Says she knows
one thing and that's you can never have a
childhood birthday again.

She's bought all this food and drink and
she's sat there filling those little plastic party
bags with Haribo and party poppers.

Admittedly I'm a bit of a state: I got blood
down my top and my eye's proper swellin'
out to <u>here</u> – so she's all 'What ya done to ya
self now Amy?' and her fella Jason comes in.
Now he's all right Jase is but he's not been
findin' work. Mum and me are mid-way
through this screamin' match an' her mouth
goes all small and tight like a cat's bum. I'm
like, after the day I've had you wanna both
shut your faces! He's livid with me: 'Your
mum's havin' a bad week.' 'She's always
havin a bad week that's why I take my sister
to school you nutter!'

Mum gets depressed and cries a lot. She says
she's got too much water in her. She cared
for my nan before she passed, and I'd say
things ain't really been the same since then.

Jase says: 'Calm down – we come up with a
plan. We'll do another car boot sale and use
that money to pay off the payday loan that
paid off the loan shark…' and I'm just sittin'
there like – WHAAAT? Sometimes, y'know,
sometimes, I'll defend my family to the
death but I gotta say it, sometimes I'm cut
real deep by the sense that maybe we are,
maybe we are like…life's losers.

'cause I love 'em, I do: in another life they'd
be like proper little entrepreneurs throwin'
ideas around. Like the time Jase borrows
his brother's van and we all drive out to
the tip and scavenge on it for stuff we can
sell at a car boot. I see my little sister, with
big gardening gloves on, and my family's
there, like, stepping over sharp rusty stuff
just looking for any shitty stuff we can sell on
– that is proper pikey I know you're gonna
think.

But Mum's like, so happy the day we do
the car boot. Sat there, in a folding chair
arrangin' all the knicknacks we have to sell
in her zip-up fleece, like some antiquer off

the telly, with a flask of tea, she's proper in her element.

She like, bloomed that day... I think she'da loved a shop of her own you know.

So they're in the kitchen telling me this plan to go to the tip again but I'm sweatin' vodka and my heart feels like it's gonna bust open. And I just flip: I tell her she's a moody depressive bitch, and I just lost my job and I can't take any more of their pathetic schemes, and why can't they make ends meet like everyone's else's family? Why can't they just stop bein' fuckin' losers?! And now my little sister's come in to see what the racket is and she's cryin' on account of the blood on my top.

Mum's upset now, says I'm all disrespect – but I'm a proper mouthy cunt to her.

'cause you know what? Maybe I prefer it when she's mad at me, maybe 'cause it feels like she's got some life in her, maybe seein' her angry feels better than seeing her so fuckin' sad all the time –

But this time her and Jase are like, final straw, that language around your sister, you wanna speak like that then you get your

own roof over your head. FINE! I say.
FUCKING FINE!

This int the whole truth because what I've
missed out for the sake of not alarmin' the
old bird is – the burglary. The <u>burglareeeez.</u>
So in reality I just casually say to her, yeah
I got kicked out 'cause of my language. Sob,
sob.

And I tell her I cried all night which is a lie
'cause I ain't cried since I was a baby an'
then I went to the newsagents this mornin'
and there's some rooms to rent, but they all
sound massively dodge. But then I spot this
yellowed ad for a rented room in a house
with 'An elderly lady.' Glenda. So that's how
I got here, I says to her.

'Oh don't be so bourgeois, gel!'

Did you just cuss me?

*'The room's not for <u>rent</u>. I ain't no private
landlord!'*

What you mean it ain't for rent?

*'The existence of private property for one-tenth of
the population relies on its non-existence in the
hands of the other nine-tenths.'*

Is that an answer? Either it's for rent or it
ain't?!

She grabs my sleeve. I'm like: back off! But
she's lookin' at me like she's gonna divulge
the biggest secret known to womankind.

*'I trust you to see the parlour. I can't go upstairs
yet!'*

And with that she drags me to the front
of the house, I'm still holdin' my cup and
saucer, and we go into the drawing room.

And it's dark, at first I can't make out the
silhouettes – there are stacks, stacks, the
room is filled and there's a bed in the corner,
but it's not dirty, it smells of beeswax polish,
and she's saying *'Sorry about the décor but say
that for me, I am spotless clean, spotless clean,'*
and I think sweet Jesus, this is the final straw,
she's one of them hoarders!

But no – she draws the curtain back and it's
only fuckin' BOOKS!

Books everywhere like she's the amazon
fuckin' ware'ouse!

I mean proper precarious like skyscraper
stacks with little gaps and alleyways through
the room for her to pootle about from one

end to the other! Barely any light gettin' in from the bay window: what a fuckin' nut bar!

You read all these?

She purses her lips and lets out a little whistle. *'PhoOOeeeeoooo-oooo'* And she smiles mischievously.

'I nicked 'em.' she says with a shrug.

You nicked all these? I nearly spit out my tea.

'They were going to either burn them or store them in a damp spot, so I took the liberty. You're not a loser my girl, not until you've truly lost something.'

Who you callin' a loser?!

'My dear, beloved, Mark Twain opened that library in 1900!

Then this council come in the night at 2am and strip the place, take down the commemorative plaque, take out the books and furniture, murals painted in the thirties, and then the other libraries were closed, one by one, and each time I caught the bus and came home with a few in my bag.

Every old bugger in this road has got a few hundred books stacked up. Hidden away, waiting until you lot want them back. It's our legacy!

We're keeping 'em stored until such a time when they are safe again, until you lot are safe! You wanna tell me you never nicked anything?'

And Mrs Glenda turns round to look at me, silhouetted by these great stacks of books.

I'm like, fuck me: now the biddy's psychic. She seen right through me!

After the pub INCIDENT, before I go home… I wake up in Swanny's car, slumped in the front seat. He's lookin' at me with something like disdain. I realise we're parked in a road I don't know. I've got like, the feelin' of dirt under my fingernails. My knuckles are swellin' up proper. Swanny points to this darkened mews house. And he goes: 'They're away for two weeks, I been casing the joint and the knobs don't have a system.' By that he means an alarm.

And he's all like, there's scaffolding out the back on next door, you can slip through a back bedroom window. He passes me his thermal gloves. I got hands like Monster Munch when I put 'em on. 'E gives me the mag-lite.

'I just been in a scrap, Swanny! What if I lose my balance?' An' I dunno. I only got myself to blame 'cause it's like right now

I feel like…really on my own. Maybe I'm
seekin' this last bit of approval from him.
Like – you might think I'm just a teenager
an' all but I know it's like, an all-time-low.
Y'see, we done six houses together in the last
four months. I ain't proud of it, I certainly
ain't now.

So I get out. Slowly, aching to fuck, and I
unlatch the side gate of next door's, and get
over the fence via the scaffold out the back
like he says.

I climb over to their back bedroom. And
it's a dud extension, my Stepdad would say.
Someone's just whacked an old bathroom
window in, instead of a bedroom one. And
the frame's rotten so I give it a little nudge,
and another, and then the top little window's
open. This is why Swanny wants me to go in,
'cause his arse'd never fit through. So I go in,
head first. Like a stealth fuckin' ninja.

It takes something, to launch yourself head-
first through a window. You gotta tumble
clear of the furniture. So I move some
ornaments and I leap through like a fuckin'
cat. I don't knock nothin' over: I land, silent.

And I stand up in this bedroom.

And that's when it happens.

You'd think I'd be used to it by now! I need
to evacuate my bowels. I get on opening
doors until I find the bathroom. I race to the
bowl to shit myself, I only just make it!

Thas why, you know – that is why some
burglars have a dump or leave a patch
of urine in your house? It's not always
vindictive like. You shouldn't feel like they
was doin' it to rub your face in it so to speak
– it's not necessarily a sort of ha ha fuck you
I done a shit or a piss on your carpet – nah!
It's often genuinely 'cause you're caught
short! Burglars shit themselves from the
adrenalin. And even Swanny and me, we still
need to go every time we do a house.

But this is the first house I done on my own.

And I am – excuse the pun – shit scared.

So I've done my business and I go through
the drawers. I find some decent rings, I find
an ipod Nano. No money, and no laptops.

I think, I'm givin' up, my heart is still thum
thum thumpin' in my chest, so I go back to
the back bedroom. What the fuck! There's a
face.

I shine the torch. I go ice cold.

A man is standin' in front of me. I'm paralysed. I shine the micro beam full in his face. My heart is going ooch-ooch: tryin' to get out. What do I do? 'E's twenty, thin in the face. He's in army togs. Starin' at me. Ain't modern army – it's old army. Too big for him. Cap under his arm. Short creamed hair. 'Uhh?' But he smiles at me, like real… kind. Like…he's a boy, hopeful? Swear to god I don't take my eyes off him, I'm like: 'crack his jaw' – but next thing I know? He's fuckin' gone!

I come to and I'm looking in the bedroom mirror. I realise I been sat on the bed for AGES! It's so quiet in this house.

And the battery's flickering in the torch, making shadows over the walls. And I've let go the jewellery but I forget the ipod's still in my glove. I climb up onto the windowsill and hurl myself back out the window.

The cold night air sorta hits me in the face. And it smells good.

I race along the scaffolding back the way I came; a dog barks somewhere. I see a fox trotting along the back row of sheds, god they can leap can't they? Little fuckin' ninjas!

I get down through next door again, out
through their side gate, and run – out onto
the street.

Swanny's in the car, sunk down low,
pretending to be asleep. I know he's seen me
coming.

'What you runnin' for?' is all he says, real
vicious, as he starts the car. We drive off.

When we pull up outside my estate he cuts
the engine. He looks at me.

'So what'd you get?'

Nothin' I says. 'You what?' Nothin' I says. I
dint – I couldn't. He goes ballistic! 'Did you
shit?' Yeah. 'And you dint nick nothing?'
Nah.

I remember I have got the ipod up my
sleeve. And somethin' goes between us,
like, I know he knows, but he's lookin' so
disgusted with me and I realise he's not goin'
to search me to check if I nicked anythin'
'cause actually, he don't wanna touch me
any more. And suddenly, that is fucking-A-
all-right by me. I'm not doin' this again.

'Can you walk?' I look down at my body.
I know now I been kicked in the kidneys.

I nod. 'Get out then.' I don't need tellin'
twice, I open the door. I get out. Except
holy mother of christ, I am seizing up,
my ribs, my stomach, all of it hurts like a
motherfucker. I am proper battered in. I
throw him the mag-lite and slam the door.
Loud. He drives off.

And I know, that I won't really – see him
again? And sure enough, you know, he's
moved on. And I think, some other poor
girl's probly bein' trained to ninja burgle for
him, and that's the bit that breaks my heart.

So the truth is that durin' the shouting match
with Mum and Jase, my sister finds the ipod
in my coat pocket. And it's there with no
headphones, and no packagin'. And I start
to say it's not mine but Jase goes fuckin' ape
sayin' he's heard I'm hanging with Swanny
and I am not to associate with that man, and
I'm a bit overwhelmed maybe, 'cause I keep
thinkin' yeah well he was the only mate I
had left!

And so I broke the proper biggest rule of
honour my family has. You don't steal. Not
big or small, you don't steal. Not a pint of
milk, not a fiver, not a light finger in a coat
pocket in the hallway, and you certainly
do NOT go breakin' and enterin.' My own

people, all three of them, suddenly we fall
silent, and I see that they are ashamed.

Mrs G's not lookin' at me now. She's lookin'
through one of the books.

'We're thieves, the pair of us!' – I say. No
response. 'I cannot believe you stole all them
books!' She shrugs. Moves along the stack. I
done it now, she's judgin' me like all the rest.
So I get – provocative.

'Libraries – they're not much use to us now,
are they? I mean you got internet caffs for
that. Pretty redundant really. First world
problems.'

Oooh yeah! She blows her little lid at that!
*'Libraries are the cornerstone my gel! Course they
want to shut' em, there's nothin' for sale! They're
emblematic of all that is good about civilisation –
free knowledge! I bettered myself with those books.
You hold a library book in your hand? You're
holding bare trust! You're holdin' the means to
revolution. And who cares if now we need crèches
and computers? Chuck us all in together!'*

And now she squares up to me – wags her
boney-ass finger up in my face. And I think,
you come any closer! I ain't above deckin'
you –

'Ohhh yeah! You're terrifyin', my gel! But not in the way you think. There's nothing more terrifying than a teenager with something to say! You mark my words gel, you'll be running this country! Even if you're too pig ignorant to see it now!'

Fuckin' call <u>me</u> PIG IGNORANT?

Oh fuck! She's gone a bit pale!

You all right? Don't you fuckin' drop on me! But she goes:

'Who's upstairs?'

No one's upstairs Mrs Glenda, no one. It's just us.

And she looks disappointed. *'Well I can't go up now, I can't go upstairs yet, can I? You come back whenever you like.'*

Come back? Not only have I done an A1 job of convincing her I ain't fit to be her tenant, reckon I nearly killed her!

Fuck me, mate! I do <u>not</u> wanna murder on my hands tonight! So I'm like er, perhaps I better make peace with my people, you know?

She just smiles, and sees me out. I race back
to Mum's, tail between my legs and beg for
my final <u>final</u> chance.

But look, I <u>did</u> hustle at Mrs Glenda's. I
dunno what possessed me but I did my
sleeve trick and shwwooooom hoovered
something up it – I pilfer this little figurine?
Later I realized Mrs G had a whole
collection of what she called her Worcester
and her Dresden ladies. And that first day
I take this little white porcelain gel with
a parasol, standing on a clump of daisies,
almost like – not to nick it, not at all –
fucking china figurine, nah!

Because! This is the weird-ass bit. I bring it
back!

She int surprised to see me. Just starts
bangin' on as she mops the place, and
muggins here can't just watch – next thing I
know? I'm fuckin' dustin' as she chats shit!

*'Now here's the trouble with livin in a terrace
in London my gel: Next door on the left got pest
control in for the mice at Christmas. And so the
mice migrate to you on the right. So we all got the
same Pest Control Man in.*

*I've never heard a man say the word poo so many
times! He comes into the kitchen and he goes.*

*(Imitates cockney Pest Control man.)'Yeah well I
pulled off the kick boards unda ya units and it's
absolutely chocca wiv POO. Absolutely chocca
wiv POO. I found POO all along underneaf the
cabinets and POO under yor cooka, and POO
right down inta the cella. Fing is when you see so
much POO Glenda, you know they been here for
some time like. So I cleaned out all that POO and
–* 'and Mrs Glenda is proper pissin herself
over the mouse man and we're both doin' an
impression going 'POO! Absolutely chocca
wiv POO yor 'ouse is!'

So I go back to her, once or twice a week
at first. Each time I get roped into cleanin'
something like a fuckin' skivvy.

*'Young thing like you oughta be out gallivanting
around with boys, or going to the pictures.'* Nah,
I'm just stayin' out of trouble! But there was
nowhere else I wanted to be more in them
days.

To be fair when she thought I was polishing
I was usually readin' the paper upstairs. I'd
come down and she'd say:

'Who's upstairs? Who's upstairs?' All excited
like, with her blue eyes shining, pale blue
like her Wedgewood plate collection, and I'd
say, no one Glenda, no one, it's just us.

And she'd look disappointed. She'd sigh: *'We been in this house for one hundred and thirty-eight years.'*

But one day, I bring a copy of *The Mail* newspaper into the house and she flips the fuck out. I'm like 'calm down you gonna have a heart attack' – it's the dementia sometimes she'd get a bit agro with me: *'You dare bring that filth into my house!* I'm like, this is an overreaction!

'This is dangerous material! You ain't got no superiors and you sure as hell ain't got no inferiors! You hear me?'

I'm like, fuck you, you old trout, yellin' at me! I'm off! I go out the front door and slam it. BAM! And then I stand on the step and think oh shit she ain't locked it behind me will she be all right? But fuck her! I storm off in a huff…but of course, I'm back next day. And she's cooled off again herself.

She's back bangin' on about how with a bit of chivvying along I could start a party that loves the country. I'm like, yeah alright, you're already bullyin' me into retaking my exams, you think I'm cut out for university?!

'University? I'm talkin' politics my gel!' Oh yeah, silly me, I'm a voice of the people, me!

But she goes: *'Only thing you're born without is a sense of deservedness my gel.'*

Oh, well – I musta just missed the fast-track to politics, now how exactly does one break into the posh cock club, girl like me?'

'You just need – as my Louie used to say – less bollocks, more balls!' And I laugh.

'No, I'm deadly serious: you got backbone.' And she prods me in the back to make me sit up straight. After that we try to come up with a girl version of that. I was like, how about 'Less pussy more vag?' And she goes: *'Less of the lip more of the…'* And we proper piss ourselves laughing.

'You're a people person, and that qualifies you above all else for the strengthening of democracy. You kids wanna be <u>more</u> angry than you are; No one to vote for? DIY it, my gel!'

And she punches her little fist in the air.

'Single failing of the Left, the death of them, was stopping caring. Simple as. One thing they used to have over the Right was to see everyone as people. Now they like to talk ethics my gel, they like to talk. But you can only be compassionate with a person if you see them as your equal.

You come in 'ere that first day with your black eye
and split knuckles, and I thought, that's ma gel!
That's the future right there and she don't even
know it.'

I liked that she don't feel sorry for me. Total
opposite!

Cheeky little fucker realises if she talks about
my Mum to me I get a bit antsy, and clean
the place top-speed in a right sweat!

I'm not ashamed to say it – on my visits
I've lifted her in the bath a few times. And I
dunno. I mean she really has no one. She's
really on her own, sort of thing.

One day I'm sat on the bog next to her while
she washes, and she says: *'Read to me.'*

I ain't a fuckin' illiterate but I never been
brilliant at reading out loud. She sighs as I
read! Keeps me in my place well an' truly!

She makes me get the dictionary open on the
cistern to test me on the words I don't know.

I complain, 'I get readin' facts but what's the
point reading literature? Fillin' my head with
middle-class twonk?'

'Middle-class twonk?!'

Ohhhhh shit…!

*'Readin' expands the mind, it means you walk
in other people's shoes, and that's radical, that is,
stories is radical!'*

So I'm lookin up the word 'proletariat' like
a fuckin' mug and a black and white photo
drops out of the dictionary. I go ice cold. I
can't breathe. It's the man I saw durin' the
burglary.

*'Oh that's my Louie in uniform. He's injured
during service. Nine months he's in a hospital
out there. By the time 'e comes back he can recite
Das Kapital. I meet him at the station and I'm
almost…ashamed…to walk along wiv 'im! He's
in a stained overcoat ten times too big. How thin
'e is!*

I open the bathroom window to let the steam
out, I sit back down. I still got the photo in
my hand.

*'He'd gotten shrapnel in his spine and they had
taken the coccyx out. They couldn't take any more
or he woulda been paralysed for life. He had an
open wound for oh, must've been two years before
it dried up. They give him a silver badge to wear
'cause of the wound, and he says 'I ain't wearin'
no Mickey Mouse badge! I wanna forget what I
done!'*

I feel a bit sparkly, I lean forward off the loo
and put my head between my legs.

*'Say what you like about the Communist Party.
I think that hope saved my husband. He had to a
do a lot of soul searchin' to forgive himself. You all
right?'*

Yeah. Yeah.

*'Seen the worst of the war and we could still have
each other in stitches. Ah, that's what you want
my girl, a feminist man, one who thinks you're the
funniest girl in the world!*

I un-crumple the photo, smooth it out. So
you're Louie. Wanking Louie, you Commie
old bugger!

*'We liked the way the state was goin' after the
war! People say Glenda there was no golden age,
the fifties was stiflin' but oh, imagine the hopes!
Imagine the NHS built afore your eyes! And then
before you know it you think…where did that…
when did that…the whole world's been skewed
and nothin's the same…'fore you know it…
you're stuck halfway up the stairs an' you can't
remember…whether you were goin' up…or comin'
down…!*

One day I come down from upstairs getting
some blankets for her. And she's at the

bottom of the stairs and she has her little arms outstretched to me, and she wants me to dance with her!

'I got two left feet, mate.' But she's trying to teach me some old dance move, bless her she comes up to about here on me. And she looks up at me: *'Who's upstairs? Tell me what you saw?'*

And so this day I think, right. I'm gonna get creative with the truth!

Well. Alright. Upstairs a couple of like, rainbows, have crystallized in the attic and a purple cloth sun rises from giant geraniums, and someone has sewn a tapestry from stars…and kids' hairclips and meteor pieces and tomato vines…and it pictures a distant land and they have lacquered the landing carpet with penguin feather oil and golden syrup, and it looks like the yellow brick road, and there's a washing line propped up by a cartoon anvil…(I'm getting' into my stride now!) and a giant harp…and pegged along it is sea urchins, sticker albums…and prescriptions…and star anise, and…there's a draught from drowsy elephant eyelashes, batting through the skylight, and this makes the harp sing, every now and again, a song you haven't heard since you were a baby, and at the top of the stairs is my diamond-encrusted writing bureau filled with preliminary sketches of the dream machine I am building, and a pipe that smells faintly of vanilla pods. And skulls.

And I pause, pretty bloody proud of my epic storytelling powers.

But she just goes:

'Ah well,' she sighs. *'Forgot that little lot was up there. But WHO is up there?'*

No one, Mrs Glenda, I was bullshitting you! And she sighs again. After alla that!

What'm I meant to tell her? Yes actually I feel a bit of a <u>presence</u> here sometimes, maybe it's your old man's ghost again. This ain't the creepy bit neither.

I read up on it but it seems there ain't many rules with senile dementia. I get the chills on a regular fuckin' basis, let me tell you – 'cause she stops suddenly, like she's seen something. Definite.

She looks into the corner of the room and goes, in this little voice – *'Dad?'* And she smiles, like she's comforted. This thing like she's crossing over, back and forth, into other – times. Or other – places.

And I see that now, it's like the going of
her is a kind of, fuck me I don't know – she
keeps going and seeing these things she finds
beautiful, and coming back, bangin' on about
her family or babies like really, she has a
foot in both worlds. Like she's able to cross,
back an' forth, like that's just what senility is,
like, a bit, beautiful.

So yeah she grew more senile.

I get lumbered with a lot of literal shit. I
wipe her arse a few times.

Cobwebs send her into a rage. She gets
more obsessed with cleanliness and has
me standing on step-ladders whipping the
cornicing with a feather duster. *'Thas it!
Thas it, whip 'em down! Whip the buggers!'*
Sometimes I'd be like, I ain't your fuckin'
skivvy!

Like one time she goes to me, *'I got a box of
sixteen different kinds of furniture polish in a little
box in the Stairs Cupboard. The Stairs Cupboard.
You gotta know which polish is for what, there's
beeswax, wood, metal, mirror polish – don't mix
'em up.'* And I'm like, I won't mix 'em up
because who needs sixteen kinds of fuckin'
polish? Who polishes?

Until one day I go round with a bit o' good news, and she's stuck in her bed in the front room. And the place is hot and stinks of shit. And I sit with her. And she looks so tiny.

Over the year she gave up dyein her hair though I offered – and now it's pure white, I realise. It's gone thin and her scalp is sticky. And she's so frail. I tell her I passed my 'A'-levels. What do I get as a well done? She points to a new stack. Stuff on Suffragettes, revolutionary women, radical women, women activists, poets, pilots, pioneers. *(Imitates GLENDA shrug.) 'There's a bit of a theme.'*

She's in and out of sleep that day. She has that same photo of Louie in her hands, and she thrusts it out to me:

'What did he lose his coccyx for if it wont a new state that took care of its people? I'd blow up parliament if I could. I'm gonna die and look what they done to my country, I dint work my fingers to the bone in munitions, I dint have my own dear love turned into a killer just to have bourgeois capitalists take over and crush our most vulnerable!'

She dint never get out of bed again, really. Next day I just sit with her. She's not talkin' much at all by now, just readin'. But she pipes up: *'I got it, Amy. Less twat more cunt!'*

Uh, fuckin comedian you are, I says.

Anyways, I sit here and we're each reading in silence, and she's making these tiny little airy farts, pffooof they're going, pfffoooof, she has no idea and I don't say nothin'… and we have a cup of tea and I eat all the bourbons…and I hold onto her tiny little hand as I turn my pages, and she's so small she feels like a bird in my hand. Something's fluttering there.

And I dunno what it was about library books but we'd both developed real funny tastes, like, as a break from coursework I used to flick through books on British Isle Birds and I'd gotten well into George Eliot who's a woman – and through the basics with Latin which made her laugh. *'Not so chippy now, eh? Workin'-class girl knows her Latin!'* On her pile of 'to read' was *The New Plagues, Grow Your Own Drugs* and *High Speed Trains!* Ah we had a right laugh we did, always peering over a book to tell the other some fact.

'Amy – says 'ere if you plant marijuana you're to make sure the soil ph is 6.5 to 7.5 as high acidity makes the plant male: a highly undesirable trait!' And we'd proper piss ourselves at

any random ass fact we could lay hands on. Dicks, right pair of dicks!

But I can say now, she was my friend.

Anyway, she dies on me: she kicks the bucket quite peacefully. And I ain't scared or anythin'. She's been seein' quite a few people in the corners of the room, smiling away, and at one point I swear she says: *'Hello Val!'* and now Val was also my Nan's name. Mum's Mum.

And you'll think me morbid, but. When she passes away I take her book from her hands, close her eyes, and I finish *High Speed Trains* before I phone the nurse.

Following day I get a call from Mrs G's legal bloke. Won't tell me on the phone, I gotta go <u>see</u> him. This solicitor hands me an envelope and inside is the front door key, the Yale. And a note in her handwritin' that fuckin' says: 'HAVE A PARTY!' And typed instructions that to loosen up a bit of capital I could sell the parking space out the front of the house but she'd like me to keep the rest of the house if I can. The legal bloke's like. 'You do know this property is worth two million pounds?'

I go back to the house in like, a daze. I sit out the front on the curb for hours…til the sun's

goin' down, and I look up and down the
street. And. Street's empty.

Alls I can think is I really oughta build some
shelves with breeze-blocks inside to stop
the spines being damaged. And maybe I'll
catalogue the lot, get a little stamp pad and
lend them out? She didn't say when I should
give them back, she said I'd know, she said
I'd figure it out, and to be honest with you I
haven't got a fuckin' clue – what'm I meant
to do, sit in there alone, Lady of the Manor? I
keep thinkin' how she said a library building
is common property. An' you can change the
whole social character of a private buildin' –
you can free it.

Two million fuckin' pounds!

But maybe – maybe I did something good
in my life. I can hear her now gettin' on at
me: *'What they'd like more than anything is for
gels like you to stay silent.'* She said: *'The only
place for silence is a library.'* She said maybe
I wanna think about gettin' some dreams. I
don't dream, I says to her. *'Use your bloody
imagination, gel? S'all it takes.'* I ain't got one,
I says.

Street's quiet. Sun's settin.'

And that's when I do it. My feet are jus'…
carryin' me…that's when I knock for

everyone. I go door to fuckin' door to invite this whole street to Mrs G's funeral. Some say are you her Granddaughter and I say <u>fuck no!</u> But I point back and I say:

(To lose the emotion AMY shrugs.)

We been in that house for one hundred and <u>thirty-nine</u> years.

I say I heard from Mrs G that a lot of people got books stored up…and would we maybe…call me a stupid cow but would it be a fuckin' idea if we maybe stuck 'em all together in Mrs G's house as a kind of… public…community…<u>lendin' house</u>. And another old gel goes: 'You mean a library?' Yeah I says I ain't fuckin' ignorant, a library is what I'm on about.

Mrs Glenda'd requested to be buried on top of Louie and not beside him, she'd said that to me with a wink.

A few elderly neighbours turn up for the funeral service. Afterwards I stand looking down into the grave. Her on top. I throw some dirt in, but I don't feel nothin.'

Next fuckin' day? This whole street's been galvanised! There's fuckin' pushchairs all lining the hall and people're building fuckin' book shelves and heftin' crates of books in.

Next thing I know my own mum's on the doorstep with a massive fuckin' tea urn – sayin' yeah why don't you live upstairs as the caretaker and open the place for a few days a week at first and we'll do little membership cards and have a kitchen for teas and kids can run in the garden and...I can barely breathe...you're mistakin' me for a 'people person!'

End of the day I got members from the whole o' Willesden! Mum says I should have a party the following week, a Grand Opening, to get to know all the members.

But I dunno. That night I'm sittin' with the dictionary in the kitchen and it feels. It feels like maybe I don't want crowds in here. Maybe I want some space.

I start cleaning like a mad fuck. I vacuum, I dust. I actually run out of things to clean. I could do a polish!

So I finally go in the stairs cupboard. *The Stairs Cupboard!* And sure enough there's this wooden crate got sixteen fuckin' different polishes in it, ones for wood and brass and metal, and I'm thinkin' 'Yes, yes Glenda, I better not mix 'em up or there'll be 'ell to fuckin' pay!' And that's when I see it. Wrapped in newspaper she's taped brass polish to it 'cause clearly she still thinks I can't fuckin' read the tin. I unwrap the paper and inside is this brass plaque. It's the brass plaque the council's heavies ripped off the library wall. Fuck knows how she's got her little mitts on it. It says MARK TWAIN. AMERICAN AUTHOR. OPENED THIS LIBRARY IN 1900.

I throw it across the room. I throw it because what am I meant to do? Fuckin' polishin? Fuckin build a fuckin halfway house or something? I got problems of my fuckin' own!

So I give this brass plaque a fuckin' Frisbee 'schwick!' of the wrist. It flies, whacks the kitchen doorframe, takes the paint off, bounces, and falls on the floor. And then, well. I ball my fuckin' eyes out. I polish it til I can see my face in it.

So…it's on the mantle. I ain't nicked it. And I ain't doin' a grand unveiling. It's over there.

I gotta reiterate, I'm just the caretaker, not some pillar of the community. Deal with your own shitty nappies. This is what I'm sayin. If people wanna use this as a headquarters, plan protests, be political, our door's open: but I ain't a saint, not at all, I'm like…a full blown arsehole, most of the time.

'Cause I did something bad, the day Mrs G died.

Just before she passes away, she says to me *'Don't be scared.'* 'I ain't scared!' I say. *'Not you, them! You're gonna terrify 'em my gel! All this beautiful anger my gel…it's gonna be very useful!'* For what? *'You stay angry my flower! Oh, would I could see it. You're gonna dream, you're gonna rise up!'* I said I ain't gonna rise up, I'm gonna muddle through like I always do. But she ignores me, and asks, like bloody clockwork, *'Who's upstairs? Who's up there?'*

And this time, I'm getting a bit emotional, for god's sakes.

I s'pose I've grown attached to her. So I'm ashamed 'cause – I shout. I fuckin' shout at her don't I? Fuckin' makin' me breathe in her shit, fuckin' sloggin' doin' her housework and wipin' her arse, fillin' my head with books and ideas? So I lose it, I fuckin' shout at her –

I say:

I don't bloody know! I don't know nothin' do I you stupid fuckin' biddy?! I don't fuckin' know! I ain't got the fuckin' answers! Maybe it's Jane bloody Eyre!

And suddenly she yells: *'Yesssss!'*

She says, *Jane's up there!'* and she smiles, and says: *'Who else?'* And I says oh, shit! Well, there's Oliver, Oliver Twist…and Madame Bovary…and Jude Fawley. And she smiles and says: 'And Tom?' Yes I says and Tom Sawyer and Silas Marner. And Mrs Dalloway, and Lolita, and Huckleberry Finn and Paddington Bear, and on and on, *'and Anna… Karenina?'*

<u>Yeah</u> I says, why not, and Anna Karenina!

And I never, never seen someone look that proud – of me. I never seen human faith like that in my life. I realise she felt like, I'm a fuckin' fraud reassurin' her like that, cause she felt like she could finally let go – an' I say don't you dare, don't you dare fuckin' let go!

She fuckin' lets go, then and there, because she thinks the future…is <u>safe</u> –

The last thing she whispers is: *'We're gonna be all right my gel.'*

We're gonna be all right.

(AMY smiles, and then smiles again, with courage.)

The End.

OTHER CLARA BRENNAN TITLES

Bud Take the Wheel, I Feel a Song Coming On
9781849430760

Theatre Uncut: A Response to the Countrywide Spending Cuts
9781849430630

WWW.OBERONBOOKS.COM